My First
Color by Numbers
and Shapes

Illustrated by Anna Clariana

Written by Moira Butterfield

Designed by Anton Poitier & Ben Potter

BARRON'S

First edition for the United States and Canada published in 2018
by Barron's Educational Series, Inc.

All inquiries should be addressed to:
Barron's Educational Series, Inc.
250 Wireless Boulevard
Hauppauge, NY 11788
www.barronseduc.com

ISBN: 978-1-4380-1143-1

Date of Manufacture: June 2018
Manufactured by: Shenzhen Caimei Printing Co., Limited

Printed in China
9 8 7 6 5 4 3 2

Puzzle and color!

This book is packed with lots of fun coloring puzzles. You need to figure out the puzzles to color the pictures.

There are questions to answer on some of the pages, too, and a few pictures to color however you like!

The puzzles get a little harder toward the end. Don't worry if you get stuck. The answers are at the back of the book.

Tip: Use a pencil to write your answers to the questions. Have fun!

Do the math to color me in!

Do the math to color me in!

1+4= 　　1+3= 　　5-4=

2+1= 　　4-2= 　　3+3=

I used ☐ colors to draw a b___er__y.

Color the amazing magical bird.
Make up a name for it.

1 2 3 4 5

This is a _____ bird.

Color the garden flowers.

Color the rounded petals yellow.

Color the 3-sided petals blue.

Color the leaves green.

Color the wacky monster's house.

I counted ☐ windows.

Color the monster's funny face.

My monster is named _____.

Color the patterns on the little lizards sleeping in the sun.

stripes

spots

zigzags

How many lizards? There are ☐ lizards.

How many fish can you see in the sea? Color them any way you like.

I counted ☐ fish.

Color the jungle and find the hidden animal.

m
j
m
m
m
j
k
l
k
k
l
l
k
j
j
l
k
l
m
k
k
k
k
m
m
j
l
m
k
l
m
l
m
m
l
m

j   k   l   m

I found a t i g e r.

Color under the sea and find the hidden animal.

o   p   q   r

I found an o c t o p u s.

Color the picture to find the hidden treasure.

a b c d

I found a c r o w n.

Color the silly aliens and give them names.

Color the racing cars and cup.

Which car is winning the race?

Color the magic castle.

I found a k i n g and q u e e n.

Color the picture to find the nighttime animal.

1 2 3 4

I found an o w l.

Color the picture to find a superfast machine.

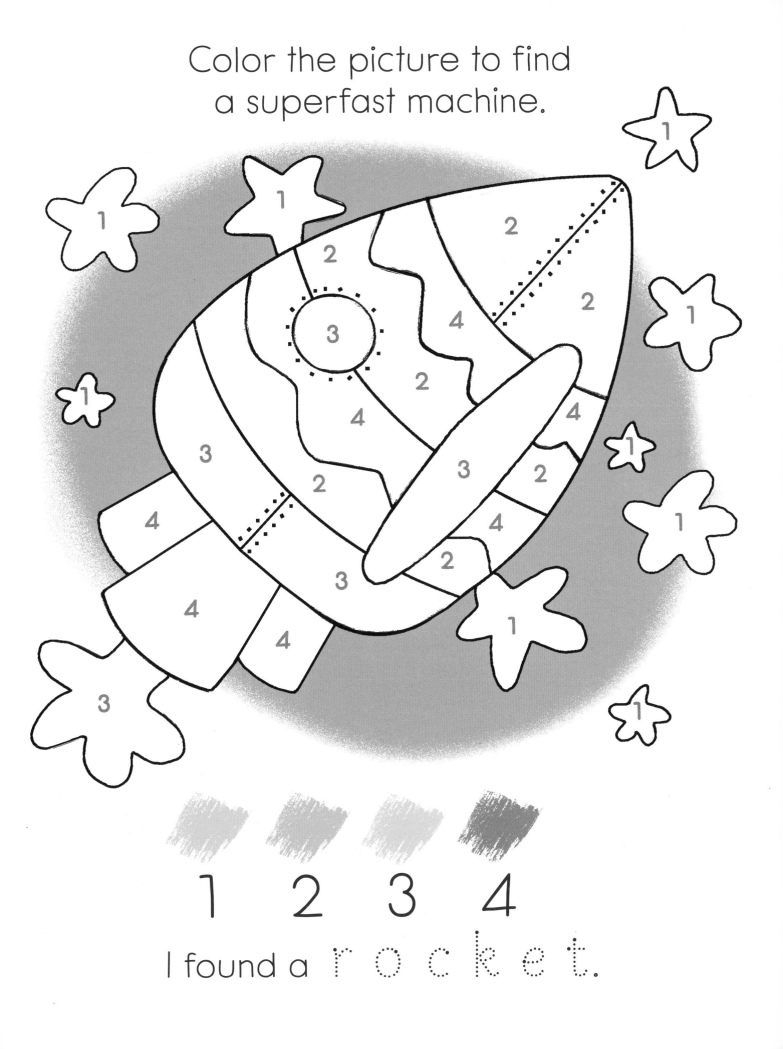

I found a r o c k e t.

Match the ships to the right pirates.

The pirate went to his s_ _ p.

Color the beach.
Then count what you can see.

I found ☐ sandcastles, ☐ umbrellas, and ☐ shells.

Color the pets.

Check the animals you can find.
Which one is missing?

Cat ☐ Dog ☐ Rabbit ☐ Parrot ☐

Color the toys.

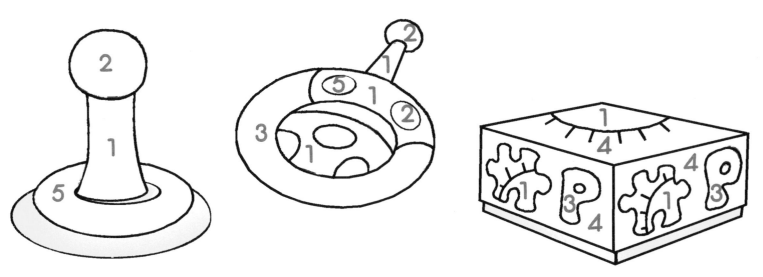

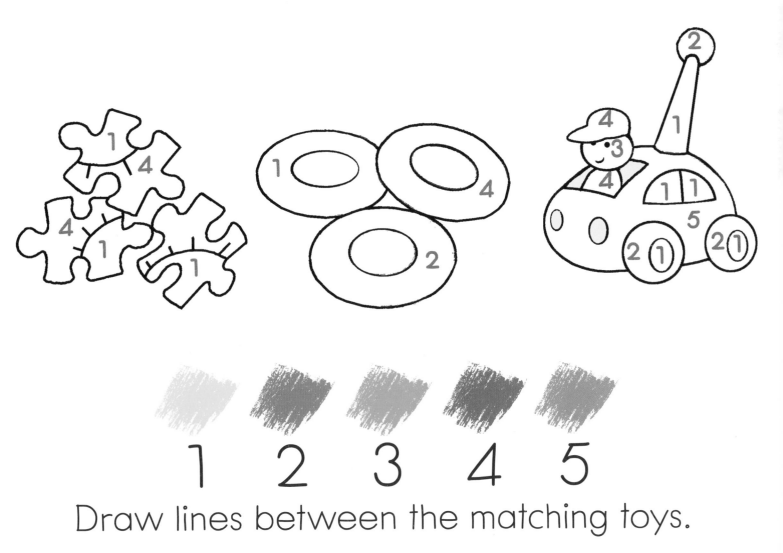

Draw lines between the matching toys.

Add the numbers to color the birthday cake. Then use your red crayon to light the candles.

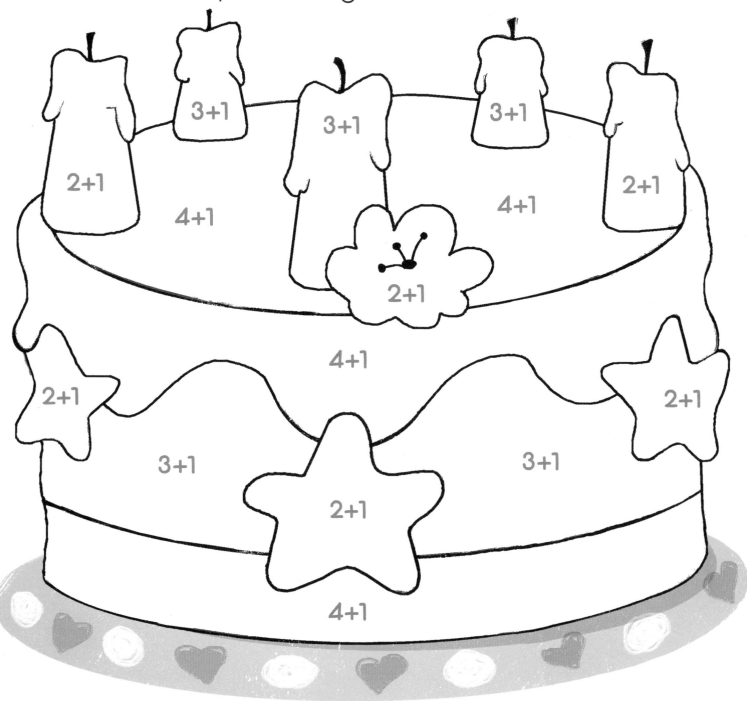

3   4   5

Count the apples to color the farm.

How many sheep can you see? ☐

Add the numbers to color the pirate's treasure map.

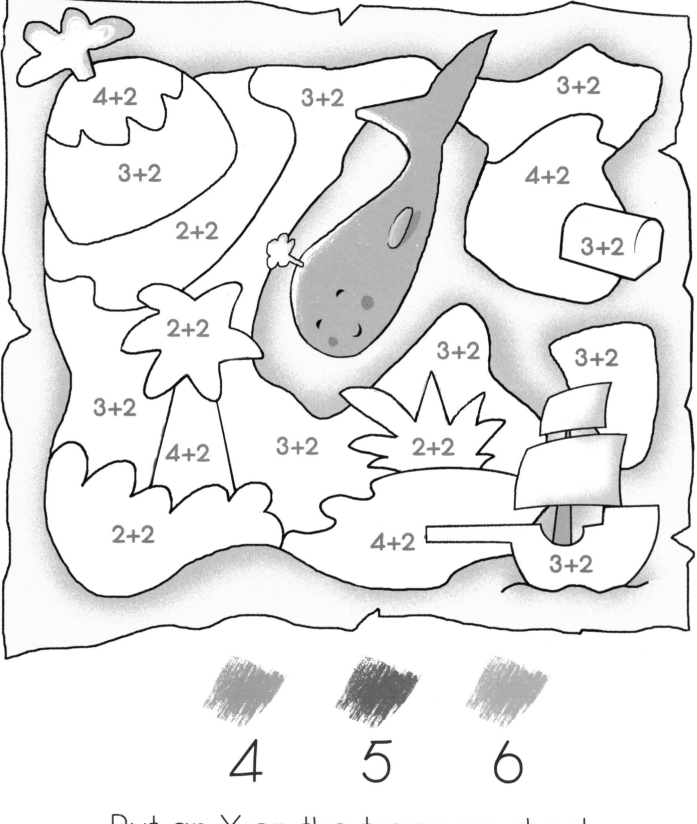

Put an X on the treasure chest.

Add the numbers to color the city buildings.
Then color in fireworks however you like.

2+2

3+2

2+2

4+2

3+2

2+2

4+2

2+2

3+2

2+2

4   5   6

Add the numbers to color the explorer's jeep. Then color the jungle as you wish.

Color outer space.

Would you like to live in space?

Color the funny aliens.

Draw lines between the matching aliens.

Add the numbers to color the mermaids.

There are ☐ mermaids.

3   4   5   6

Color the juicy fruit jigsaw.
Then circle the missing piece.

1 2 3 4

Color the rainbow jigsaw.
Then find the two missing pieces.

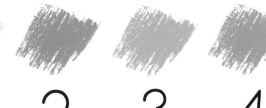

1   2   3   4

Color the picture frame and draw
your face in the middle.

Make sure you are smiling!

Color the garden and draw a
garden animal in the middle.

What will you draw?

Finish drawing the octopus.
It needs 8 arms. Then color it in.

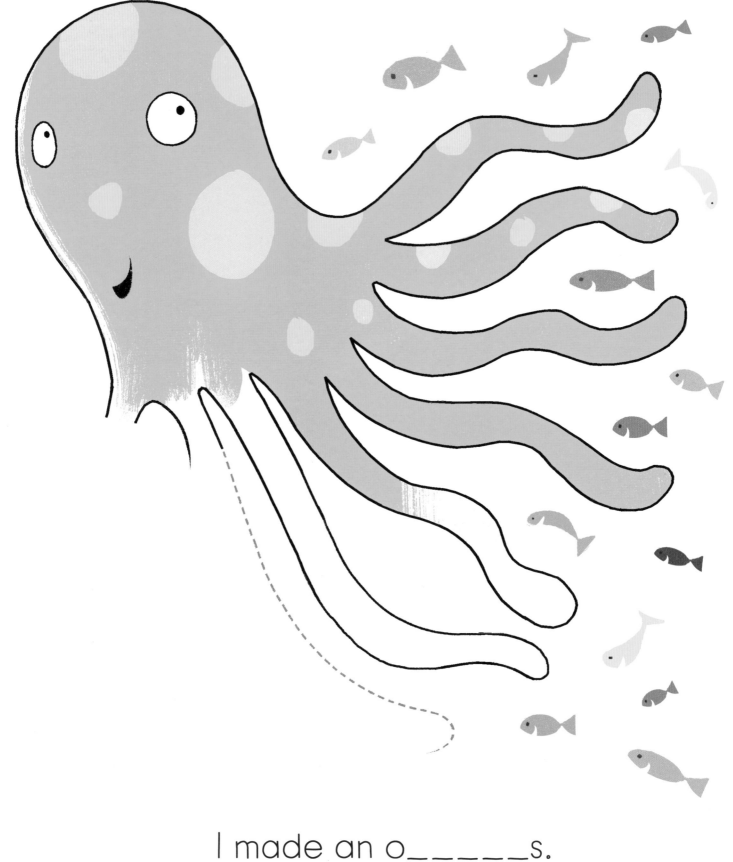

I made an o_ _ _ _ _s.

Color the frame and draw the first letter of your name in the center.

Can you help the children find their bouncy balls?

Draw lines to match the balls and the children.

Color the fairies however you like.

Draw lines to match the fairies and the doors.

Add the numbers to color me in.

6   7   8   9

Each morning I go cock-a-d____e d__!

Add the numbers to color me in.

6 7 8 9

I like to h__s.

Add the numbers and color the forest.

5   6   7   8   9   10

I found a c_t hiding in the forest.

Complete the drawing by connecting the dots.

1

6

2

5

3

4

Color me however you want.
Write something in the bubble.

Complete the drawing by connecting the dots.

Color me however you want.

Add the numbers and color us in.

6   7   8   9   10   11

I found a swimming t____e.

Color the unicorn and choose a name.

My name is _____.

Who is hiding here? Color the picture and check the answer.

a b c d e f

elephant ☐ hippo ☐ crocodile ☐

Who is hiding here? Color the picture and check the answer.

h   i   j   k   l   m

penguin ☐   bear ☐   monkey ☐

Color the sleeping cats and dogs in pink.
Color the leaping cats and dogs in orange.

Use any color for the rest.
I found ☐ sleeping cats.

Match up the dinosaurs.
Then finish coloring them in.

Draw your own dinosaur here:

Color the castle any color you wish.

I counted [   ] flags.

Color the ice cream sundaes any color
you wish. Draw two more below them.

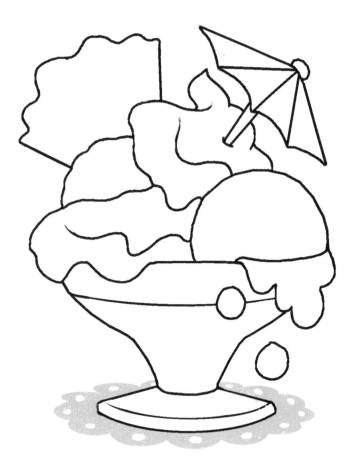 

I counted [　] ice cream sundaes.

Draw another cupcake on the plate and color the picture.

I ate one cupcake. There are ☐ left.

Draw one more car in the parking lot and color the picture.

My mom drove one car. There are ☐ left.

Add the numbers to color the sails.

5   6   7   8   9   10

I counted [ ] boats.

Add the numbers and color the scene.

5 6 7 8 9 10

I counted ⬜ bicycle wheels.

Add the numbers and color the scene.

6   7   8   9   10   11

I counted ☐ animals.

Add the numbers and color the scene.

6   8   10   11   12   13

I found ⬜ tractor.

Add the numbers and color the scene.

5   6   8   9   10   12

I found ☐ tigers.

6 butterfly

4

3

10

tiger

octopus

crown

red

king queen

owl

rocket

ship

1,2,3

parrot

3

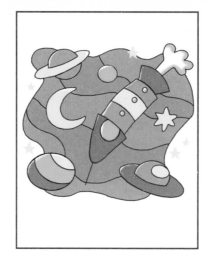

3

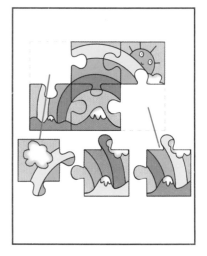

octopus

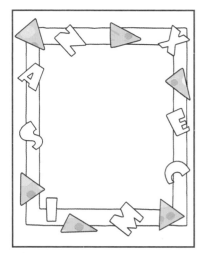

cock-a-doodle doo

hiss

cat

turtle

elephant

monkey

2

6